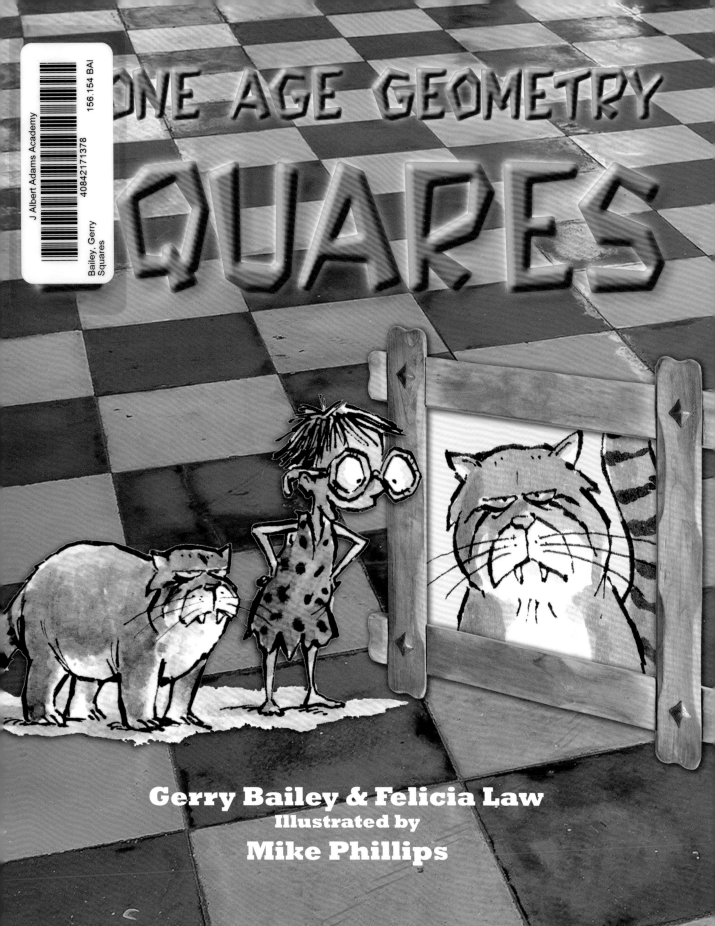

STONE AGE GEOMETRY
SQUARES

Gerry Bailey & Felicia Law

Illustrated by
Mike Phillips

Crabtree Publishing Company
www.crabtreebooks.com
1-800-387-7650

Published in Canada
616 Welland Ave.
St. Catharines, ON
L2M 5V6

Published in the United States
PMB 59051, 350 Fifth Ave.
59th Floor,
New York, NY 10118

Published in **2014 by CRABTREE PUBLISHING COMPANY.** All rights reserved. No part of this publication may be reproduced, stored in a retrieval system, or transmitted in any form or by any means, electronic, mechanical, photocopy, recording or otherwise, without the prior written permission of the copyright owner.

Printed in Canada/032014/MA20140124

Authors: Gerry Bailey & Felicia Law
Illustrator: Mike Phillips
Editor: Kathy Middleton
Proofreader: Anastasia Suen
End matter: Kylie Korneluk
Production coordinator and
   Prepress technician: Samara Parent
Print coordinator: Margaret Amy Salter

Copyright © 2012 BrambleKids Ltd.

Photographs:
Cover - Sophie Bengtsson, Title - Sophie Bengtsson
Pg 2 – Gerard Lacz images / Superstock Pg 3 – David M. Schrader Pg 5 – (t) www.padfield.com (b) John Kasawa Pg 7 – (t) auremar (m) Dario Sabljak (bl) PerseoMedusa (br) trouvik Pg 9 – (t) Morphart Creations inc. (m) polartern (b) Tim Roberts Photography Pg 11 – (tl) Philip Lange (tr) Andrjss (ml) Giancarlo Gagliardi / Shutterstock.com (mr) Kamira (bl) TonyV3112 (br) Mikhail Markovskiy Pg 13 – (t) Jiri Hera (m) Dr Morley Read Pg 14 - Patrick Poendl Pg 15 – (tl) James Clarke (tr) BartlomiejMagierowski / Shutterstock.com (b) Patrick Poendl Pg 17 – (t) KROMKRATHOG (m) (b) Natursports / Shutterstock.com Pg 19 - tankist276 Pg 21 – (tl) Kornthong Jamsrikaew (m) Pep Fuster (bl) Lukiyanova Natalia / frenta Pg 23 – (t) konmesa (b) mountainpix Pg 25 – (l) Stefano Ginella (r) mountainpix / Shutterstock.com Pg 27 – bezmaski Pg 29 – (in panel from top to bottom) Stephanie Frey, apirati333, Sergey Goruppa (tr) badahos (mr) leolintang (br) Ryan M. Bolton Pg 30 – (tl) Reinhold Leitner (r) Bridgeman Art Library / SuperStock (bl) Betacam-SP Pg 31 – (tl) Natursports / Shutterstock.com (tr) Golden Pixels LLC (bl) Rob Hainer (br) Kodda
All images are Shutterstock.com unless otherwise stated

Library and Archives Canada Cataloguing in Publication

Bailey, Gerry, author
    Stone age geometry: Squares / Gerry Bailey, Felicia Law ; illustrator: Mike Phillips.

(Stone age geometry)
Includes index.
Issued in print and electronic formats.
ISBN 978-0-7787-0511-6 (bound).--ISBN 978-0-7787-0517-8 (pbk.).--ISBN 978-1-4271-8236-4 (html).--ISBN 978-1-4271-9006-2 (pdf)

    1. Square--Juvenile literature. 2. Geometry--Juvenile literature. I. Law, Felicia, author II. Phillips, Mike, 1961-, illustrator III. Title.

QA482.B35 2014   j516'.154   C2014-900426-5
                                           C2014-900427-3

Library of Congress Cataloging-in-Publication Data

Bailey, Gerry, author.
 Stone age geometry: Squares / Gerry Bailey & Felicia Law ; illustrated by Mike Phillips.
    pages cm. -- (Stone age geometry)
 Includes index.
 ISBN 978-0-7787-0511-6 (reinforced library binding : alk. paper) -- ISBN 978-0-7787-0517-8 (pbk. : alk. paper) -- ISBN 978-1-4271-8236-4 (electronic html : alk. paper) -- ISBN 978-1-4271-9006-2 (electronic pdf : alk. paper)
 1. Square--Juvenile literature. 2. Quadrilaterals--Juvenile literature. 3. Geometry--Juvenile literature. I. Law, Felicia, author. II. Phillips, Mike, 1961- illustrator. III. Title.

 QA482.B3438 2014
 516.154--dc23
                                           2014002076

LEO'S LESSONS:

MEET LEO

Meet Leo, the brightest kid on the block.

Bright, as in IQ off the scale; inventive, as in Leonardo da Vinci inventive; and way, way ahead of his time....

So that's Leo!

Block, as in Stone Age block; Stone Age, as in 30,000 years ago.

Then there's Pallas— Leo's pet.

Pallas is wild, and he's OK with being called Stone Age, too; after all, his ancestors have been around for millions of years. That's more than you can say for Leo's! You won't see many Pallas cats around today, unless you happen to be visiting the icy, cold wasteland of Arctic Siberia (at the top of Russia).

FOUR EQUAL SIDES

Leo and Pallas are practicing their army **drill**.

"Watch me!" says Leo. "I'll mark out the perfect square.

See? I take one step in this direction. Then I turn smartly and take one in this direction. Now I turn smartly again and take one in this direction. Then..."

"You turn smartly again and come back to the place where you started." Pallas shows he understands.

"Good!" says Leo. "Now it's your turn. Just 4 moves. It's quite easy."

But Pallas can make a square without moving at all. After all, he has four legs, one at each corner.

"You'll never make a good soldier," says Leo.

SQUARE

A square is a **two-dimensional**, or 2-D, shape. This means it has a length and a width.

A square has 4 sides that are of equal length. That means its length is the same as its width.

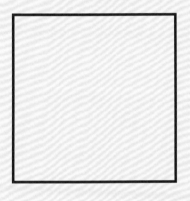

In mathematics, we show that the sides are equal using this sign /.

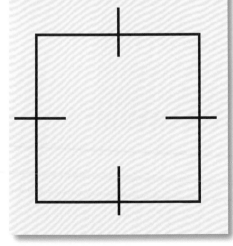

The Testudo

Testudo means tortoise in the Italian language. Roman soldiers used their shields to make a kind of shell, like a tortoise shell. They raised their shields above their heads and held them in front of their bodies. The testudo formation protected them against arrows or objects thrown by people defending a castle from the walls above.

Roman soldiers march forward in the testudo formation.

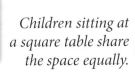

Children sitting at a square table share the space equally.

5

AT THE CORNER

"What are you doing?" asks Pallas. "Why do you need all this equipment?"

"We're planting," says Leo. "We dig holes. We put in sticks. We plant the seeds. We wait for the plants to grow."
"We?" asks Pallas. "Cats don't plant."

"I need you," says Leo. "The poles have to be joined along the top so the plants can climb up, then grow sideways.

So if you climb up the poles, you can tie the string along the top."

"Just tying then?" says Pallas. "No digging. No putting in poles. No planting. Just tying string along the top."

"Tightly," says Leo. "You must pull it tight and keep it straight. You must keep the string at a right angle to the poles."

"You know what?" says Pallas.
"You do the planting...

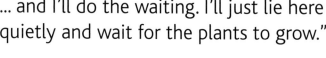

... and I'll do the waiting. I'll just lie here quietly and wait for the plants to grow."

6

SQUARE

A square has 4 corners that are the same size and shape.

Everywhere the sides of a square meet, they form an angle known as a right angle. The size of an angle is measured in degrees, which is written with the sign °.

A right angle has 90°.

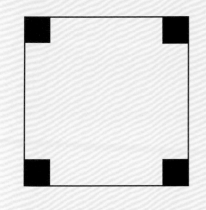

A builder uses an instrument called a steel square to measure a perfect 90-degree corner.

This square frame shows all four 90-degree angles.

Small twigs grow at 90 degrees from the main branch.

In vineyards, grapevines wind along supporting posts as they grow. This way the fruit will grow at 90-degree angles and get lots of sun and ripen easily.

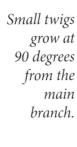

GRIDS

"You"re standing in the middle of the street," says Leo. "I would watch out if I were you."

"Street?" says Pallas. "I can't see a street."

"Well, not now perhaps," agreed Leo, "but there will be one very soon. This is my town plan."

"A town?" asks Pallas. "You're building a town?"

"Yep!" says Leo. "See? The main street goes here leading into the town square. Then these two side streets join it at right angles. Pretty cool, huh? The town will be called Leoville."

Pallas is impressed.

"And the square will be called Pallas Square," says Leo. "After you."

Pallas is super-impressed.
"So we'll be famous," he says.
"All the people who live in this town will know about us."

"Ah!" sighs Leo. "People! The people thing may be a bit of a problem..."

GRIDS

A grid is a series of lines that cross each other at right angles. They cross at 90°.

Grids are used to plan maps. They are also used in geometry and other kinds of math.

COORDINATES

A coordinate is a number that identifies a particular point on a grid. Numbers are placed along the base and up the side of a grid. To locate a point, you need to follow one number upward from the base and another number across from the side. The location of the point is where the two lines meet.

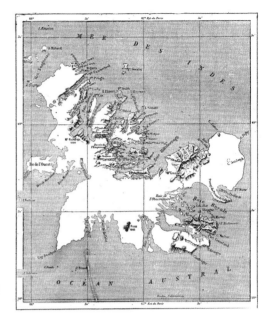

A map marked with a grid makes it easier to find places.

Fields are often laid out in a grid formation between straight lines.

The streets of this town are built in a grid pattern.

9

IN THE SQUARE

"Fancy that!" says Pallas. "A square named after me—Pallas Square.

It will be the center of the town.
Roads will lead in and out of the square.
People will stroll in the sunshine and stop to chat. Cats will be welcome.

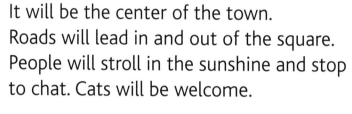

There can be a fountain in the middle.
And four statues, one in each corner of the square—statues of me.

Each week, people will meet at the market in the square to buy and sell.

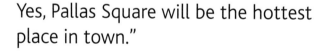

Yes, Pallas Square will be the hottest place in town."

At night, the square of Djemaa El-Fna in Morocco is packed with storytellers, magicians, snake charmers, and food stalls.

The Grand Place is the central city square of Brussels in Belgium. Every two years in August, an enormous "flower carpet" is set up there.

Trafalgar Square in London is the most famous city square in the United Kingdom.

New York's famous city square, Times Square, is filled with video screens, **LED signs**, and flashing lights.

A perfect square lies at the heart of the town of České Budějovice in the Czech Republic.

Tiananmen Square is in Beijing, China.

11

MAGIC SQUARES

Leo is busy with numbers.
He is so busy with numbers he doesn't notice
that Pallas is busy with bones.

Leo must solve a puzzle. He has 9 numbers
to put into a grid inside a square. They must be
arranged so that they will always add up to 15,
whether he adds them across, down, or on a diagonal.

Pallas has his own puzzle to solve. He has 45 bones
to be eaten over the next 9 days. According to his
diet, he must eat a different number each day.

He can eat lots one day but fewer the next.
And he can eat them in any order as long as
he never eats more than 15 every 3 days.

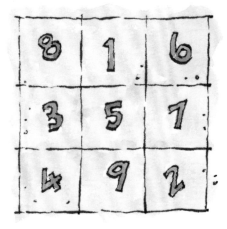

They both get
there in the end.

And it looks as if
they both get the
same result.

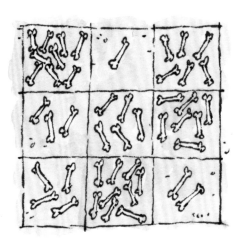

In the game sudoku, numbers must be filled into blank squares on a grid so that each full row and full column adds up to the same number—45.

LO SHU

There is an ancient Chinese story that tells of a number puzzle called Lo Shu. Four thousand years ago, the banks of the Yellow River flooded the land around. The people made sacrifices to the river god, but the floodwater stayed.

Then, one day, a turtle climbed out of the water. On its back were nine squares, arranged in a grid on its bumpy shell. In each of the squares, there were marks that matched the numbers 1 to 9. Whichever way the numbers were added the sum equaled 15. The people made 15 offerings to the river god, and the floodwater went down.

This, say the Chinese, was the origin of the magic square.

A Yellow River tortoise

8	1	6
3	5	7
4	9	2

MAGIC SQUARES
Each number from 1 to 9 appears only once in a magic square.

If you add up the numbers in any row, the total will be the same as the total for any column or any diagonal.

ON THE WALL

"It's time," says Leo, "that we got ready for the Art Show."

"Gosh!" says Pallas. "An Art Show here in the cave? What art are you going to show?"

"All this," says Leo sweeping his hands around the walls. "But people have just scribbled all over the place like children. I need to make it look more organized."

"Do people pay good money for this?" asks Pallas. "I mean, even a cat could do better paintings than that."

"It's ART," says Leo. "We just have to make it look like art, that's all."

And they do!

Delicate Japanese art is often set in simple elegant frames.

RECTANGLES

"What's the problem?" asks Leo.
"I want a new bed," says Pallas. "My old bed's got lumps in it, and it's not big enough."
"That's because you're growing," says Leo.
"Growing fatter. You eat too many bones."

Pallas looks at the beds. Leo suggests he get a hammock, or a futon, or a sleeping bag to lay on the cave floor. "Something simple," he says.

But Pallas wants a real bed—

A single, a double, even a king size!

Or a grand four-poster bed.

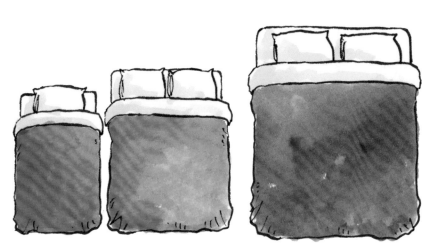

RECTANGLE

A rectangle is a four-sided shape like a square, but, unlike a square, its four sides are not all the same length.

Only the opposite sides of a rectangle are of equal length. Opposite sides are also parallel to each other, which means the lines are always the same distance apart.

Every corner angle is a right angle. A right angle measures 90°.

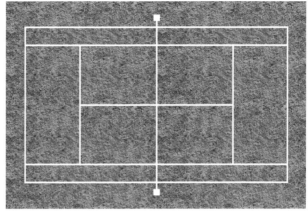

A tennis court is made up of eight different rectangles plus the rectangle that is the entire court.

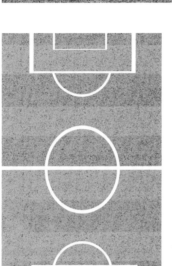

A soccer field is a huge rectangle. It is marked with other rectangles that show where players may or may not go.

A soccer field is a rectangle that measures 50 to 100 yards (45.7 to 91.4 m) wide and 100 to 130 yards (91.4 to 118.8 m) long.

17

PARALLELOGRAMS

Leo is making a bridge
across the stream.
He seems to need lots of
large, flat square slabs.
It's hard work!

He piles them high in the water.
The sides must be straight.
It's hard, wet work!

Now he needs lots of even
larger, flatter slabs to make
the walkway along the top.
It's *really* hard, wet, heavy work!

And he needs to cut poles
for **handrails**. The rails must
be perfectly lined up. They
must be exactly parallel.
It's really tough work!

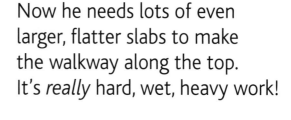

Pallas knows he should help,
but he'd rather sleep!

Rope bridges

Bridges made of rope or vine might have been the first kind ever invented. Some are just a length of rope to walk on while others have a narrow plank.

These bridges need a rope handrail for the user to grab on to, or they'll be thrown off as the bridge swings. Handrails can be made safer by adding more rope strands to the walkway like a kind of web.

A PARALLELOGRAM

A parallelogram is any 4-sided shape that has opposite sides that are parallel.

Parallel sides are sides that are an equal distance apart.

The sides never meet.

A square is a parallelogram.

A rectangle is a parallelogram.

A shape like this, called a rhombus, is a parallelogram.

TESSELATION

"It doesn't fit," says Leo. "Look, I'll explain it again.
Look for a shape that fits exactly alongside this one.
No cracks or holes, get it?

Then find another that fits alongside, and so on."

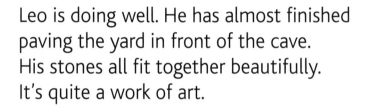

Leo is doing well. He has almost finished
paving the yard in front of the cave.
His stones all fit together beautifully.
It's quite a work of art.

Pallas is helping, but his pieces of stone
don't fit together at all.

The sides don't fit!
The corners don't fit!
The edges don't fit!

Pallas has made a piece of crazy
pavement— and it's quite a work
of art, too!

SHAPES THAT TESSELLATE

Tessellation describes the way shapes of the same kind fit together snugly so that there is no overlapping and no gaps. Also, the points where the shapes meet always looks the same.

Only three shapes do this.

squares

triangles

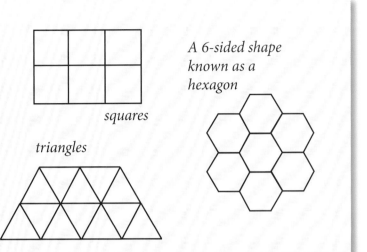

A 6-sided shape known as a hexagon

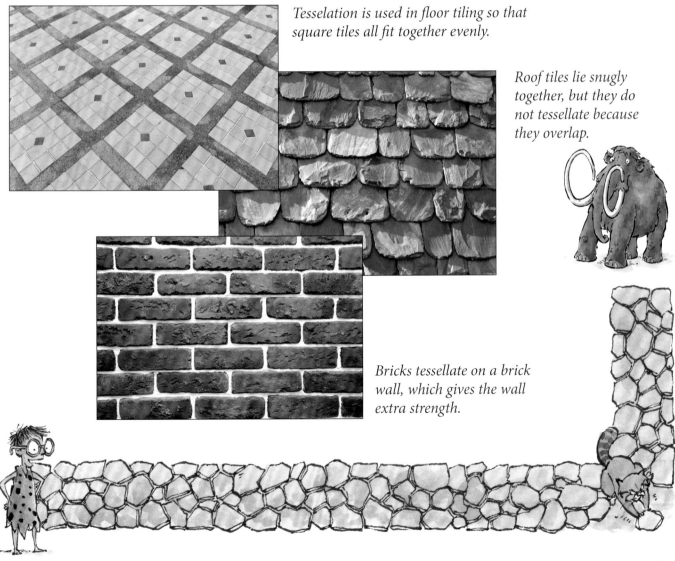

Tesselation is used in floor tiling so that square tiles all fit together evenly.

Roof tiles lie snugly together, but they do not tessellate because they overlap.

Bricks tessellate on a brick wall, which gives the wall extra strength.

MOSAICS

"Don't touch!" says Leo. "What are you doing?"
Pallas is scratching at the wall. He has managed to pull
one piece of red stone off already, and he is working
hard at another.
"Pallas!" warns Leo. "Don't touch!
You're destroying the mosaic."

Leo looks around. There is a guard. He is there to stop
visitors from taking bits of the mosaics,
but he seems to be asleep.

"It was loose," says Pallas.
"I just tidied it up."
"Leave it alone," says Leo.

"Hold on," says Pallas.
"I need a piece of blue."

"Come on!" says Leo. But it seems that
Pallas wants a piece of yellow as well.

"Now," says Pallas. "I've found all these pieces,
so I'm going to make my own."

But Leo tells him to put them all back!

So he does!

Mosaics are made of small pieces of colored stone like tiny tiles. They're used to create pictures, just like a painting.

Roman mosaics

The ancient Romans decorated the floors of their homes and temples with mosaics—patterns of colored stone that are fitted together. Some are made up of thousands of tiny pieces. They show animals, Roman gods, people at work, or simply beautiful patterns.

Some of these mosaics have been uncovered by archeologists hundreds of years later.

Mosaics can be used to create pictures of people as well as patterns and scenes.

23

THE SQUARE DANCE

"Wear this!" says Leo. "And this!"
He pushes a hat onto Pallas's head and ties
a frilly apron round his waist.
"OK," he says. "Let's dance!"
"Let's what?" shrieks Pallas. "Cats don't dance!"

"I know," says Leo. "But you have to help me out.
I need four couples to do a square dance, one couple
on each side of a square. You and I must be the first couple."

"But you're still missing three couples," says Pallas.
"Yes," says Leo. "We'll have to move around a lot,
so no one notices."

"First" says Leo, "we skip across the square.
Then we swing each other around.
Then we skip back across the square.
That's couple number one done."

"That's it?" asks Pallas.
"That's square dancing?"

"No," says Leo. "Now we cross over and
start all over again as couple two..."

"Hold on..." says Pallas. "I think we need
some more dancers...."

DIVIDING THE SQUARE

The diagonals of a square are lines drawn from one corner to the opposite corner. There are two diagonals in a square.

The diagonals of a square are of equal length.

They cross in the exact center of the square.

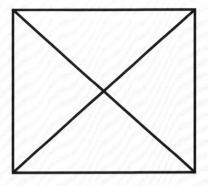

They divide the square into four identical triangles.

You can also divide the square with two straight lines that form a cross in the center of the square. They make four identical squares.

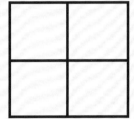

The Union Jack

*The Union Flag, or Union Jack as it's sometimes called, is the national flag of the United Kingdom. Its **intersecting** lines are the result of combining the flags of England, Scotland, and Northern Ireland.*

Square dancing

A square dance is a folk dance with four couples, or eight dancers in all. The couples are arranged in a square, with one couple on each side. Couples 1 and 3 face each other and are the head couples. Couples 2 and 4 are the side couples.

Traditional square dance uses about ten to thirty different moves. The moves are called out by a "caller." The dancers do what they are instructed to do in time to the music.

Lots of dances use a square formation, such as this one from Mongolia.

RHOMBUS

"You are always so busy making things," says Pallas.
"Why don't you take a vacation?"

"Good idea!" says Leo. "Let's go fishing."

"Don't we need a boat?" asks Pallas.

"Yes," says Leo. "We'll build one."

"Don't we need a paddle?" asks Pallas.

"Yes," says Leo. "We'll make one."

"Don't we need a fishing spear?" asks Pallas.

"Yes," says Leo. "We'll sharpen a **flint** and make one.
Come on, there's lots to do..."

"You know," says Pallas,
"maybe I'll just go and buy the fish."

DIAMOND SHAPES

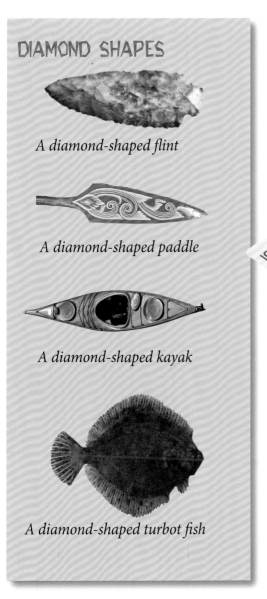

A diamond-shaped flint

A diamond-shaped paddle

A diamond-shaped kayak

A diamond-shaped turbot fish

A precious stone is cut in a diamond shape.

Diamond shapes are used on playing cards. In many games, diamonds are considered lucky cards.

RHOMBUS
A rhombus is a four-sided shape where all sides have equal length. In addition, opposite sides are parallel, and opposite angles are equal. The rhombus is often called a diamond.

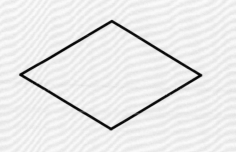

Snakes such as the rattlesnake, use their diamond shapes to help them blend into their surroundings. This helps them stay safe from enemies ands allows them to creep up on prey undetected.

FUN AND GAMES

Artists enjoy working with square shapes. Look at these works and see how squares form an important part of each painting.

A square is a strong shape, supported by a right angle at each corner. You will find square shapes in many buildings, toys, and pieces of equipment. Squares are also often used to divide an area in games and sports.

Mondrian was a Dutch painter who worked with strong square lines and colors.

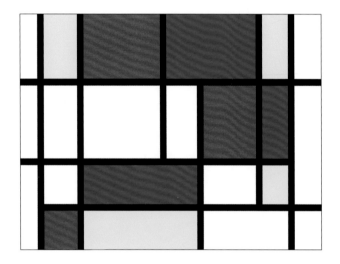

Paul Klee made this painting of buildings using square shapes with triangles.

*Op art, also known as optical art, is a style of visual art that makes use of **optical illusions**. This sphere is made of square shapes.*

Hurdles are square-shaped frames that are used in a track-and-field event.

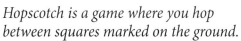
Hopscotch is a game where you hop between squares marked on the ground.

The ropes are knotted in squares on this ladder.

Chess is a game where you move black and white pieces between squares.

KITE

Leo is sending a message.
Pallas wants to know who he is sending it to.
But Leo won't tell.
"Have you got a girfriend?" asks Pallas.
But Leo won't tell.

"I'm going to tie the message to this kite.
Then I'll fly the kite high in the sky so the
message can be read a long way off."

"By everybody?" asks Pallas.

"No," says Leo. "It's in code."

"Of course!" says Pallas "It would be!"
He knows how clever Leo is.

But he wishes he could read the message.
He'd still like to know if Leo has a girlfriend!

LEARNING MORE

OTHER BOOKS

Basher Science: Algebra and Geometry
by Dan Green and Simon Basher,
Kingfisher (2011).

Mummy Math: An Adventure in Geometry
by Cindy Neuschwander,
illustrated by Bryan Langdo.
Square Fish (2009).

The Greedy Triangle
by Marilyn Burns,
illustrated by Gordon Silveria
Scholastic Paperbacks (2008).

WEBSITES

Get the facts on the square and its properties
at these entertaining websites:

http://www.mathsisfun.com/geometry/
 square.html

Find a variety of games and activities with
geometry themes.

www.kidsmathgamesonline.com/geometry.
 html

This website provides information on shapes
and their properties.

www.mathsisfun.com/geometry/index.html

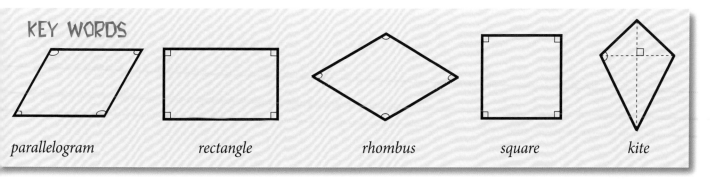

KEY WORDS

parallelogram   *rectangle*   *rhombus*   *square*   *kite*

GLOSSARY

drill The training of soldiers in military skill and discipline

flint a hard dark quartz that produces a spark when struck by steel

handrail A narrow rail to grasp for support

intersecting To meet and cross at one or more points

LED signs A type of electronic message sign made up of thousands of tiny lights called LED's (light emitting diodes)

optical illusions Seeming to see something that does not exist or that is not as it appears

two-dimensional Having, or appearing to have, length and width but no depth

INDEX